The One Philosophy

The Little Message
With a BIG Impact

Nancy Matthews

ParkerHouseBooks.com
Tallahassee, Florida

This book is designed to provide information and inspiration to our readers. It is sold with the understanding that the publisher and the author are not engaged in the rendering of psychological, legal, accounting or other professional advice. The content is the sole expression and opinion of the author and not necessarily of the publisher. No warranties or guaranties are expressed or implied by the publisher's choice to include any of the content in this book. Neither the publisher nor the author shall be liable for any physical, psychological, emotional, financial, or commercial damages, including but not limited to special, incidental, consequential or other damages. Our views and rights are the same: You are responsible for your own choices, actions and results.

To request custom editions, special sales and premium and corporate purchases, please contact **Nancy@NancyMatthews.com** or call 800.928.6928.

This book is
dedicated to
The Ones
who have been,
and continue to be,
The Ones for me.

I am honored and grateful
to be The One for you, too!

Praise for
The One Philosophy

"*The One Philosophy* is a powerful, life-enhancing book. It's the very embodiment of the saying that great things come in small packages. Following the principles set forth in this book is the way we're meant to live and experience each other. It will result in and more abundant life...for you, and for those whose lives you touch."

~ Bob Burg, Co-Author of *The Go-Giver*.

This little book, *The One Philosophy*, surely does hold a big message...the secret to a fulfilled and purposeful life is to focus on serving others first. Thank you Nancy Matthews for highlighting this important code for living.

~ Sharon Lechter, Author of *Think and Grow Rich for Women*, Co-author of *Outwitting the Devil*, *Three Feet From Gold* and *Rich Dad Poor Dad*.

"*The One Philosophy* distills and makes accessible the wisdom of all the master teachers throughout the centuries. It is a philosophy for living. It is the biggest little book I have read in a long time. "

~ Johnny Regan, Vision Coach

"After the first read, I thought *The One Philosophy* was a novel idea. The second read enticed me to consider what shifts might occur if I actually implemented *The One Philosophy*. The third time was the charm, and I was convinced. This all took place in one weekend! I am so grateful to Nancy Matthews for this life changer. In less than 100 pages, you will learn how to BE the One. That "simple yet powerful secret to turning chance encounters into meaningful connections" is now mine.

~ LaRonda Robinson, Vision for Jamaica

"What a great attitude adjustment! Such a simple shift in perspective offers such a huge payoff. I owe a debt of gratitude to the author for creating a simple, enjoyable to read tool for myself and my employees. Do yourself a favor and read it and share it."

~ Cheri Bithell, Brook & Hearth Salon

"If you want to improve your networking skills, personal relationships AND really enjoy people you meet read this book! Nancy Matthews comes from a heartfelt space and with a step-by-step approach helps you ease into that space with revealing exercises. I have implemented these techniques and it has improved my interactions with everyone I meet. There is nothing like feeling great every time you talk to someone. AND my business sales have skyrocketed because I treat each client as if they are The One because I KNOW they ARE The One! Buy and enjoy this book - your life will change for the better."

~ Lisa Montgomery, Luxurious Fishing Vacations

Contents

Preface

What was it that brought you to this book? Was it a recommendation from a friend, the cover, the title, the copy on the back cover, or just plain curiosity?

By virtue of the fact that you're reading this now, there are a few things I already know about you.

You're someone who wants to make a positive difference for yourself and for others.

You're someone who is going for more in your life and you're willing to take more action than the average person is to achieve your goals.

You're someone who understands the value of continuous learning and growth and you're willing to invest in yourself.

The promise of this book is that when you embrace and apply The One Philosophy you will experience greater levels of fulfillment, enhanced relationships and an overall increase in the quality of your life.

What you're about to learn is something so simple that its mighty power is often overlooked.

What you're about to learn is the core philosophy that I've used and applied throughout my life. Living the principles of The One Philosophy has allowed me to enjoy great relationships with family, friends, clients and business colleagues.

It has been my guiding principle in business where I have had the privilege of operating million dollar businesses and successful careers in the legal profession, real estate, business consulting, writing and speaking in many countries.

It is also the core philosophy of Women's Prosperity Network (co-founded with my two sisters), a global community providing resources, connections and consulting to women and men in business.

It is the philosophy that I've shared with thousands of people bringing them increased joy, abundance and rich rewards in every area of their lives.

It is … The One Philosophy

The One Philosophy that when embraced by you and shared with others, has the ability to transform your life and the lives of everyone you meet.

The Framework

Living the way of The One is about **BEING** The One for others first, foremost and always.

It's about taking the time to value, honor, and appreciate the people in your life.

By people I mean "all the people." Your family, friends, colleagues, clients … AND the people you meet on the street, at restaurants, supermarkets, networking events, conferences, etc.

When you live in the perfect order of things – first by BEING The One for others – that is the place from which our existence is meant to function. And --- as a result, living the way of The One then brings you the realization and fruition of your goals and dreams.

This is not because it's some magic formula that can be manipulated in your favor.

Rather, the realization of your goals and

dreams is the effect brought about by you being the cause of love, care and respect for others.

It is the natural return that occurs when you first seek to serve others.

When you begin with the pure intention of being The One to be of service and add value, that essence permeates all of your words, actions and deeds. It's the basic formula from which all other good emanates.

When you move through life with this purity of intention in all your interactions, (you being The One as the cause), the resulting effect is the realization of your vision, purpose and goals.

~ Caution ~

Your job is to be The One.
Your job is to be the cause.
The effect takes care of itself.

Consider the law of gravity. When you throw a ball into the air (the cause), you don't focus or question whether the ball will come down (the effect). You simply know and trust that it will. In fact, you can't stop gravity from having its effect on the ball.

The same is true about being The One.

The principles and stories in this book are designed to:

- Provide guidance and direction to live your life as The One for others.

- Create clarity and focus on your goals, vision and purpose. Your unique reason for being a part of humanity in this particular place and time.

- Support you in focusing on being the cause; that is, being The One.

Nancy Matthews

The Beginning

Since my early years I have believed that there is meaning and value in every interaction we have with others. That every person I meet is placed with me at that particular moment in time for me to learn something from them, or for them to learn something from me. And quite often, the learning is mutual!

Throughout my life this has been my overall approach with people, but there was a time when this life philosophy slipped out of focus. In the frenzied and hectic pace of providing for my two children as a single mom; developing my professional career and then building my businesses, I somehow forgot this essential rule of life.

And then I was given the first of many gifts to remind me. A T-Shirt from my boyfriend that read:

"The most important things in life aren't things." ~ Anthony J. D'Angelo

Fast forward a few years later. I had a meeting scheduled with a local news anchor who wanted to explore doing a television show together.

As I was mentally preparing for the meeting, I found myself filled with a heightened sense of excitement and enthusiasm about meeting her. She was "The One" who was going to help my dream of having a TV show come to life.

And that's when the realization hit ...

Why is it that this heightened sense of excitement, enthusiasm and attention tends to come about when we think we're meeting "The One?"

- The One who's going to be your next big client.

- The One who can make a powerful connection for you.

- The One who's going to give you the solution you've been looking for.

- The One who could be your next best friend, your spouse or partner.

When we think we're in the presence of The One we tend to pay extra attention, listen more intently and overall, treat that person with more respect than we would to someone who is an unknown. We seek out ways to demonstrate how much we value them through our words, actions and deeds.

What is it that causes us to treat *those* Ones with more attention and excitement?

When you think someone is The One that means you know something about them that relates to something you want. This thought of possibility creates excitement for the role The One will play in your life, bringing you closer the realization of your goals and dreams; that is, helping you get what you want.

I stopped and thought, "Wait a minute. If every interaction with others has meaning and value, why would I place a higher value on meeting someone who I thought was The One? Every person I meet has value and what better way to experience life than by treating <u>everyone</u> I meet as The One?"

And so it began, The One Philosophy was born as a reminder to:

Treat each and every person you meet as The One because they are!

The One Philosophy reminds us that the person sitting next to us is The One and our priority is to create the space for every interaction to have more value. You achieve this by being interested in them, taking the time to learn more about them and finding ways to be The One for them in that moment.

Once you take the lead by being The One

to get to know this once unknown person, by listening with ears that seek to discover who they are, eager to learn about the things that matter to them and bring them joy, you have now created an environment of care and respect that sets the foundation and safety for a meaningful connection to occur. You will find people opening up to you more quickly, sharing about themselves and asking questions and being genuinely interested in you.

It is in this space of embracing The One Philosophy and being The One that the magic and miracle of living the way of The One thrives.

The Ones are everywhere – do you now see them?

Just as the photographer adjusts their lens to see more clearly, we must adjust the lens through which we view people to see them as The Ones they truly are.

Now, here's the best part! When you begin to treat people as The One, you become The One for them by reminding them that they are important, valued and appreciated. You are fulfilling one of our most fundamental human needs, the desire to be seen, heard and valued for who we are.

When you create this feeling for the people you're with, they now become excited to be around you! When people feel good being around you, they will feel safe and more easily open up to share about themselves. From that place of connection and sharing of what really matters, the possibilities created by this powerful exchange and now meaningful connection are revealed.

"I've learned that people will forget what you said, people will forget what you did, but people will never forget how you made them feel."
~ Maya Angelou

Several years ago I was teaching a seminar in Florida on clarifying your goals. As the guests were arriving, I engaged in conversation with a 26-year old named Dan.

"Hi, I'm Nancy Matthews, it's great to meet you and I'm so glad you came tonight. Tell me a little about yourself." He shared that he was from Canada visiting his sister, Vanessa, and that she invited him to come to the event.

"That's wonderful," I said, and I asked him to tell me a little more about himself.

"Well," he said boldly and confidently, "I want to be the Manager of the Florida Panthers hockey team."

"Way to go! I love your confidence and determination," I replied.

The topic of the seminar was about creating your vision and being able to boldly state your goals and dreams. I was so impressed by Dan's confidence that I shared from the stage, "Take Dan for example. He's visiting here from Canada and when we first met tonight he shared that his goal is to be the Manager of the Florida Panthers." No sooner were the words out of my mouth when a girl sitting a few rows back raised her hand and said, "I babysit for the owner of the Florida Panthers!"

The Ones really are everywhere because we are all meant to be The Ones for each other. The question is, are you taking the time and making the effort to be The One?

You now hold in your hands the keys to the kingdom. These are the principles and practices of living the way of The One. The One Philosophy that will bring you more in every area of your life.

Throughout this book you'll learn how to embrace and apply The One Philosophy.

You'll learn how to resist the temptation to hurry through your day and miss out on The Ones who are all around you and showing up in your life for a purpose and a reason.

You'll learn how to see the best in others even when they themselves may have forgotten or never realized their own value.

You'll discover ways to find the uniqueness and sameness in everyone you meet.

You'll get to be The One who reminds people they are loved, appreciated and have great value.

Part One

Embracing The One Philosophy
Starting from the Inside Out

You've most likely already started to embrace The One Philosophy. Seeing people you meet in a new light, enjoying more positive interactions and feeling the rewards of living the way of The One.

You may be wondering:

> *"Is it possible to keep this*
> *shift in perspective all the time?"*

How do you make the time in your busy life to begin to recognize that every person you meet is The One?

How do you shift from the "don't talk to strangers" message that was ingrained in so many of us as children, to being open and excited about meeting new people?

How do you leave behind the feelings of mistrust and disappointment from being let down in the past by people who you thought were The Ones?

How do you share your message and your vision with others in a way that doesn't come across as trying to pitch them or sell them, as trying to get something from them, but rather, sharing yourself in a way that allows the inherent opportunities to be revealed?

How do you fully embrace and share The One Philosophy? Through faith and trust, one step at a time just as Lisa did...

"I was introduced to The One Philosophy by Nancy Matthews at my first Women's Prosperity Network meeting several years ago. While the theory felt very good when thinking about it, I wondered, would it really work? How would others respond to this new behavior? I thought it would be difficult to change old behaviors that have been ingrained for years in meeting and interacting with people daily. But I would try

one person at a time and give it the old college try.

I was delighted. This was much easier than anticipated! Bit by bit I kept treating each person I encountered as if they were my "One." The first thing I noticed was that I felt really good about other people and myself. In the past, when I typically would get irritated with a situation, now I wasn't looking at it from only my point of view. Now it is with more compassion and patience.

I received another great benefit almost immediately (and I LOVE instant gratification) …when meeting new people I can now remember almost every person's name! I thought I simply had a screw loose and would never master this skill. However, switching from "I wonder what this person will be like…how will they receive me?" to now thinking "I can't wait to see who this person is!" has made all the difference.

The One Philosophy has also allowed me to serve my clients completely. I remember details of our conversations because I am really listening to them, not just picking out the facts to accomplish the task at hand. I care more about them and am *doing a wonderful job on their behalf. And let me tell you – they NOTICE.*

I get testimonial letters and referrals for what I consider to be "regular service." But to them it is not regular service. Someone genuinely cares and handles the details for a perfect trip and life-long dream fulfilled. What more can I ask for than that?

And last but not least, it is wonderful to know that each time I go to the grocery store, a restaurant, or the bank, I leave happy people behind. They have been acknowledged, looked in the eye, and they know what they do is important.

Thank you Nancy for delivering this gift to me and everyone I meet. The golden thread of love is what is intertwined in the human race and holds us together. This is the thread."

~Lisa Montgomery
LuxuriousFishingVacations.com

And now, onto the principles of living the way of The One.

The Principles of The One Philosophy

These principles will guide you through the best of times and the most challenging of times. The way of The One will support you in being able to maintain an attitude of gratitude and a spirit of hope and enthusiastic anticipation despite the appearances of current circumstances, obstacles or challenges.

Begin By Remembering… You Are The One!

Yes, YOU are The One!

- The One who has been given the gift of the present. Open it with expectation of good things to come.

- The One who has unique gifts and talents

that are meant to be shared with others. Share them and BE The One to serve others.

- The One who has the power to transform every interaction by bringing feelings of love and gratitude to the situation.

- The One who has the power to make a big difference in the world. Never think that you're too small or insignificant to create a shift and cause things to change.

The following principles will support you in remembering you are The One and in being The One for others in our fast paced, demanding and hurried world.

Making the commitment to integrate these principles into your way of being will bring you rewards, joy and happiness beyond your wildest dreams.

The Principles of
The One Philosophy

T	**Principle 1:** Talk Less and Listen More
H	**Principle 2:** Hold Your Vision & Share It With Others
E	**Principle 3:** Exhibit Exemplary Behavior and Attitude

O	**Principle 4:** Own Your Life by Taking 100% Responsibility
N	**Principle 5:** Never, Never, Never Gossip
E	**Principle 6:** Exercise Your Mind & Your Spirit: Develop & Grow Daily

Principle: 1

Talk Less and Listen More

"Be a good listener, your ears will never get you in trouble." ~ Frank Tyger

Talk less and listen more and I mean *really* listen!

Being The One begins with listening. Being fully present in your conversations and keeping your focus on the other person. I know that this can be difficult at times, especially in our distraction-driven society, where we are all too often rushing through each moment so we can scratch off all the items on our "To Do" lists, hit our goals and reach the pinnacle of success. I invite you today to find success in each moment by demonstrating true care and concern for the people you're with – in your family, among your friends, with your co-workers, clients, customers and prospects.

A simple shift in perspective to being The One who *really* listens to others, will bring big rewards in every area of your life:

- Be The One in your family who truly listens to your spouse, your children and your siblings and discover a deeper relationship based upon mutual respect and appreciation for each other.

- Be The One in business who fully listens to what your clients and customers say, and be The One to serve their needs better than anyone else.

- Be The One at networking events who listens first and asks questions that allow others to share about themselves as you discover the uniqueness and brilliance of the person you're meeting.

- Be The One in the grocery store, the restaurant or the elevator who looks people in the eyes, tunes in and listens to them and actually cares about the answer they give to, "How are you today?"

Years ago, I was the guest speaker at a Regional Conference for Jafra Cosmetics and had the honor of being introduced by Ann Fetters, a veteran Jafra consultant and an amazing woman and leader. I had given Ann my bio to introduce me and was surprised and delighted when she deviated from the standard intro and shared from her heart:

"One of Nancy's greatest gifts is her ability to listen, to fully give you her attention, whether you're with her one on one or in a group with hundreds of people. When you're with Nancy, she's totally with you."

Wow, I was blown away! I hadn't realized the far reaching impact that my commitment to being a good listener had on others.

How does one become a better listener?

Here is the story of another of the many gifts I've received to remind me of the importance of listening and being fully present.

When my daughter was a teenager I would pick her up from school every afternoon. Although the school was actually walking distance to our home, I wanted to pick her up and enjoy some quality time together. As she got in the car, she would tell me about the happenings of her day. She spoke at what seemed like a thousand words a minute, barely taking a breath or a pause, while at the same time I had a thousand words a minute running through my head from my busy day at work.

On this particular day she stopped mid-sentence and said, "Mom, you're not listening to me!"

I realized she was absolutely right and although I *thought* I was listening, what I was really doing was multi-listening; that is multi-tasking with my ears!

I was half listening to her and half listening to the words in my head about what I was going to do when I got back to the office. I wasn't fully present in either conversation and it clearly was not the 'quality time' I set out to create.

That was a powerful wake-up call and I vowed that day, and still practice to this day, being fully present with her and with everyone I meet.

This habit of quality time with my daughter after school continues to this day. Even though she's grown and lives hundreds of miles away, she still calls me on her way home. I am so grateful and blessed!

"It's the little things that are vital. Little things make big things happen."
~ John Wooden

Being a great listener is one of the highest forms of respect. When you give your total attention to another person (especially in this multi-media, instant messenger world), they feel valued and appreciated – the foundations for solid relationships.

Tips for Better Listening:

- Look into the eyes of the person you're speaking with.

- Be excited and eager to learn something new from the other person.

- Resist the urge to look over their shoulder or to the side to see who's coming in the room next.

- When your mind starts to drift away from what they're saying, simply notice it and gently bring your attention back to the other person. More likely than not, the other person will have noticed that your attention drifted. Bring your attention back to them and ask forgiveness.

- If someone is speaking with you and the environment is not conducive to you being able to give them your full attention, let them know and set a time to speak with them. I encounter this often at events where there are numerous demands on my attention. In that scenario I explain, "I want to give you my full attention but it's not possible right now with me being pulled in so many directions. Let's set a time to have this conversation."

- Turn off your "Already, Always" way of listening. (i.e. "I already know what Bobby is going to say" or "I've already learned how to be a good listener" and "Betsy is always complaining about her husband" or "Bill always says the same thing.") When we enter a conversation with a pre-conceived notion of what the other person is going to say, we run the risk of missing out on learning something new.

- If you're trying to win an argument or prove your point, consider (even if just for a moment) that the other person may actually have a point as well!

I invite you now to be The One you want to meet in the world. Imagine how it feels to be met by someone who is really listening to you, is interested in what you have to say, who asks for more information and is delighted by your knowledge, your sense of humor, and your perspective. Be *that* person when you meet others and be The One who leaves the world a better place with each and every interaction because you showed up fully present, really listening and totally engaged in the moment.

Principle: 2

Hold Your Vision
And Share It With Others

Because you're reading this book, I can safely assume that you are someone who has a vision or at least has an inkling of a vision stirring within them.

What's your vision?

In the preface, I shared that embracing and applying The One Philosophy by being The One will cause you to experience greater levels of fulfillment, enhanced relationships and an overall increase in the quality of your life. Your vision, goals and desires will be realized with more frequency and greater ease.

In order for this to work, you have to create a vision for what it is that you <u>really</u> want.

Having a clear vision of what you really

want and sharing it with others opens the field of possibility for the people who are meant to support and contribute to your vision to appear. Once again, I caution you to keep your intention on cause and effect in the proper perspective. As it pertains to vision, your job (the cause) is to get clear about what you really want to achieve and to share your vision with others. Meeting the people, circumstances and opportunities that support your vision is the effect.

Vision is the driving force behind all great accomplishments. Vision inspires passion and provides the inspiration, stamina and energy to pursue your goals and achieve them. Often referred to as your 'WHY', vision also serves as the fuel you'll need to keep on going when the going gets tough.

Take some time now to get clear on your vision. Allow yourself to dream, to wish and to tap into your heart's desires. What do you want to bring into your life? Who do you want to be spending time with? Where do you want to live? What kind of car will you be driving? How will you spend your leisure time?

If you're like most people, you may find that the moment you begin to declare your heart's desires, your mind chimes in with perceived obstacles or challenges that could prevent you from having what you want. Be prepared to move beyond those thoughts, simply notice them and continue focusing on your heart's desires.

Remember to focus on what *you really DO want* rather than on what you don't want. It is often easier to recognize what we don't want, in part, because what we don't want may be what we are currently experiencing.

To activate the power of your vision and The One Philosophy stay focused on what you want to create in your life.

For example:

What You Don't Want:
   I don't want to feel stressed about my bills.

What You Really Want:
> *I want to earn $100,000 this year.*

What You Don't Want:
> *I don't want to fight with my family.*

What You Really Want:
> *I want to have great conversations with my family and have them feel safe and secure in telling me what's happening in their lives.*

What You Don't Want:
> *I don't want prospects to turn me down.*

What You Really Want:
> *I want to meet people who appreciate and value what I have to offer.*

What You Don't Want:
> *I don't want to feel rushed and overwhelmed.*

What You Really Want:
> *I want to enjoy my day with grace and ease, knowing I'll get all the most important things done.*

What do you *really* want? What's your vision?

With a clear vision of what you want, it will be easier to recognize the pieces of the puzzle being placed in your path to bring about the realization of your vision.

Remember Dan who was visiting from Canada and shared his vision of being the manager of the Florida Panthers? What if Dan wasn't clear about what he wanted or hadn't given himself permission to believe it was possible? What if he lacked the confidence to share it with me? That synchronistic moment would never have occurred.

Embracing and applying The One Philosophy in your life so that you can enjoy all the benefits it brings, requires you taking the time to know your vision, hold it clearly in your mind and to share it with others.

While I don't know the outcome of the meeting between Dan and The One he met that evening, I do know that opportunities come to those who hold their vision, act with purpose and who share their vision with others.

Are you taking consistent action in alignment with bringing your vision to life? Do you know how to effectively convey your vision to others?

Give yourself time to think, to dream and to plan. Hold your vision firmly in your mind and your heart and share it with others with passion.

In Principle 6: Exercise Your Mind & Spirit: Develop & Grow Daily, you will be given simple, yet powerful, exercises to support you in fueling your vision with passion and desire. This is the fuel that will keep you inspired, engaged and consistently in action - living as the full expression of your heart's desires.

One last note on vision – visions come in all shapes and sizes and no one vision is more important than another. The only thing that matters is that your vision comes from your heart and represents your true desires.

Whether your vision is to be the best spouse or parent and have a loving, engaged and thriving family, to be a millionaire and enjoy the lifestyle freedom it brings, to create far reaching impact on humanity or if your vision is to be the General Manager of a Hockey Team - every vision matters!

You may have heard the phrase "thoughts become things" or "what you think about comes about." I believe this to be true and further that everything that matters begins in the heart in the form of desire and passion. Then, the desire moves up into our minds to form thoughts which are expressed through words which we then turn into action to bring about our heart's desires.

Principle: 3

Exhibit Exemplary Behavior and Attitude

"Becoming number one is easier than remaining number one." ~ Bill Bradley

Think for a moment of the people who have made the greatest impact in your life. Who are your heroes, role models and mentors? What did you most admire, respect and appreciate about them? Was it the size of their wallets? Was it their flashy cars, big houses or extravagant lifestyles of the rich and famous?

While all of those material things may have caught your attention, and they certainly can be fun to have and enjoy, I bet it wasn't those things at all that created a lasting impression about the people you most admire. It was who they were, their

41

attitude, behavior and character. It was how they treated others and how they dealt with life in the face of challenge as well as triumph.

Being The One invites us to be the best we can be at all times and to be exemplary in our attitude and behavior. The definition of exemplary is:

Worthy of imitation, commendable, serving as a role model. (Dictionary.com)

Are your attitudes and behaviors worthy of imitation?

Are your actions commendable?

Are you serving as a positive role model for others to follow?

How we show up in the world, how we treat others, and how we deal with difficult or challenging situations defines our character.

Character and values are not often the topic of everyday conversations, but you bring them with you everywhere you go and into every situation and interaction you have with others. Knowing your values and guiding principles allows you to exhibit them and makes it easier to be exemplary, especially when you're faced with challenges and having to make tough decisions.

When I owned my title company, a client came in after hours to finalize a closing transaction. It was a short sale transaction, which means that the bank was willing to take less than what was owed on the mortgage loan to settle the debt. We were finalizing the paperwork to send to the bank and the client suggested adding an expense item to the transaction that would result in $10,000 being diverted back to him and he offered to give me half of the money.

"No one will know and it will just fly right through. The bank won't miss the money." There it was – my moment of truth. Although he said 'no one' will know, that wasn't the case. The truth for me was that I would know. Regardless of the fact that no one else may ever find out about it or the perception that the bank wouldn't miss the money, my truth was that it was not the right thing to do.

At the risk of losing the client, I refused to do the transaction. Would it have been nice to have an extra $5,000? Sure, but not at the expense of my values. Fortunately, the client acquiesced and we completed the transaction the right way.

Having a clear understanding of your values and your commitment to live by them makes decision making easier, especially when you're faced with conflicting desires. My conflicting desires in the situation above were: the desire to have an extra $5,000, and the desire to do the right thing.

The decision was easier to make because I was clear that my value of honesty was more important than the value of wealth.

What if the value of wealth was more important than that of honesty?

What if the value of security was more important and I believed that the $5,000 would bring me more security?

The values we hold and live by are as

unique to each and every one of us as our thumbprints. Knowing your values will support you in living the way of The One and make it easier when life presents its interesting opportunities and challenges.

What are your top values and guiding principles?

Take some time now to review the list below and circle the values that most resonate with you.

Recognition	*Learning*
Peace	*Wealth*
Honesty	*Pride*
Intelligence	*Power*
Innovation	*Health*
Wisdom	*Community*
Integrity	*Cooperation*
Spirituality	*Kindness*
Self-Respect	*Love*
Achievement	*Creativity*
Family	*Affection*
Vitality	*Freedom*
Loyalty	*Security*

Leading a life in alignment with your values and with clarity of your vision continues to unleash the power and magic of living the way of The One.

Give yourself an opportunity to deepen your connection to your values and their application in your daily life by considering the following:

From the list of values above (or others you may have added), if you had to choose one value over all the others that best describes you and/or the driving motivator for your life, which would it be?

How does this value show up in your business and/or in your life?

Reflect on a situation where you may have had to make a difficult choice, felt threatened or anxious. Can you now identify which of your core values was either being confronted or felt out of alignment?

How will you now use the awareness of your core values in your daily life?

I have adopted a set of guiding principles for my life that support me in continuously living in accordance with my values. I found this list in *The Abundance Book* by John Randolph Price and it has served me well as a daily checklist in living the way of The One.

Right Action – taking action in accordance with my values. It may not always be the easiest path but it's always the path that leads where I ultimately want to go.

Joyful Thanksgiving – remaining in a continuous state of gratitude and appreciation for all that I do have in my life and <u>really feeling it</u> – that's the joyful part!

Verbal Harmlessness – keeping my words kind and positive about others and myself. Negative self-talk can be the most damaging words of all.

Intense Love – when I say the words, "I love you," I pause and actually feel the love. When I think about people I love, I go deeper and feel my love for them by remembering details of who they really are, the qualities and characteristics that I most love about them.

Meditation – taking time each day to quiet my mind, connect with my inner spirit and the infinite source of energy and love.

Controlled Visualization – focusing daily on what I want, how I feel having attained what I want and the impact my vision has on the lives of those around me.

I keep this list in my view both near my desk and by my bedside for a consistent reminder of the way of living that supports my highest good and being The One.

"We are what we repeatedly do.
Excellence, then, is not an act but a habit."
~ Aristotle

Principle: 4

Own Your Life By Taking 100% Responsibility

This principle sets you free to be the complete creator of your life. When things are going well, this feels absolutely awesome, "Hey, look what I created!" Conversely, when things aren't going so well that usually turns into, "I didn't do *that!* Someone else must have caused that to happen to me."

The truth is that our current circumstances and everything we are experiencing in our lives, the good, the bad and the ugly, are the results of choices we've made and actions we've taken in the past. The greater truth, however, is that as you learn to treat every experience (both the good ones and the not so good ones), as learning opportunities, your true power is revealed and you'll find yourself having more good ones than bad ones.

Consider your current circumstances. Have you been faced with any of the following situations?

- Is your business slow and there aren't enough clients paying for your products or services? While it's easy to blame the market or the economy for your financial condition, the reality is that there is something you are bringing into the business that's causing the slow down. Take a look at yourself, your behavior and attitude towards customers, examine your sales cycle or system (or lack of a system), review how your products and services are (or aren't) providing the best solution for your market segment. Fixing the problem is much easier when you know the challenge and the solution come from you.

- Are you overweight or out of shape? Was this caused by someone forcing you to eat all that ice cream or blocking the door to the gym so you couldn't get in? You have choices every day that either bring you closer to optimal health or further away.

• Are you lacking in friends, romance or a social life? It's not 'everybody else' who is causing this. What actions have you taken to be a better friend, get out into the dating scene or join clubs or charity events where you'll meet people with similar interests?

Just like the school child who doesn't turn in their homework and says, "The dog ate it," we are each solely responsible for the current condition of our lives.

By no means am I discounting the challenges and upset that sickness, loss or personal tragedies may bring. Those things do occur. What I am suggesting is that the severity of how they impact your life is directly related to how well you have prepared prior to them occurring.

Have you cultivated trusted relationships and been there for others in their time of challenge? Have you saved for a rainy day? If you've taken those types of actions before the challenge arises, it will lessen the blow and the severity of its impact on the quality of your life.

Sure we can try to blame the way we were raised or some horrible experience we had in the past for what's happening in our lives today, but how does that serve us now in living the life we truly want?

It is said that the loss of a child is the most unbearable loss of all. My niece lost her son in a tragic accident at the age of 17. After years of suffering, self-blame and almost losing her own life in the process, she has now been able to transform this loss.

Here is her story:

The One Philosophy

"Number One" Son

Eddie was in a coma for approximately
10,000 minutes…
and for some reason those 10,000 minutes,
and his passing,
and those saddest of minutes that followed,
became more time consuming than actual
time itself -
as if those minutes were all the minutes that were
ever going to be…
because there was so much more I wish
I had shared with him
the 10,000 minutes before.
I understand what it's like
to be suspended in time…
to be so incredibly regretful-
to be so sincerely sorry that there isn't one
minute left-
just 60 seconds more…
60 seconds to have, to share, to smile,
to embrace,
to gift words of love or adoration or gratitude and
to know that sentiment has been received.

And so through his life and his death
my son Eddie remains The One.
The One who taught me
that I need not choose to let fear or pride or
awkwardness stand in the way of loving,
or feeling or letting those I love know how
precious they are to me -
not for 10,000 minutes or 10,000 seconds
or that one single blink of an eye...
Eddie's beautiful spirit is my forever reminder to
begin each day as if it is on purpose
and to live each day as if it was my last.
To let those I love know just how much they
are cherished and those who are kind how truly
appreciated they are.

LIFE IS A GIFT...
Accept it, unwrap it, and
experience all of its joy, now.
~ felice cellini ~

Taking 100% responsibility for everything that occurs in your life will give you more control and when you have control, you get to direct the course of your life.

In his book, *The Success Principles,* Jack Canfield shares of his revelation on the power of taking 100% responsibility. When Jack went to work for W. Clement Stone, a self-made millionaire worth 600 million dollars (and that was in 1969!) he was asked, "Jack, are you taking 100% responsibility for your life?"

"Well, I think I am, but maybe I'm not," Jack replied.

What an interesting question!
Are you taking 100% responsibility for your life?

When we start from the place of knowing that we are responsible for our lives, we can then claim our power to create whatever we want. Here's what Mr. Stone then said to Jack:

"Taking 100% responsibility means you acknowledge that you create everything that happens to you. It means that you understand that you are the cause of all your experience and if you really want to be successful, and I know

you do, then you'll have to give up blaming and complaining and take total responsibility for your life. And that means all your results – your successes and your failures. This is a prerequisite for creating a life of success. It is only by acknowledging that you have created everything up until now that you can take charge of creating the future you want. You see Jack if you realize that you've created your current conditions, then you can un-create them and re-create them at will."

(Excerpt from *The Success Principles* by Jack Canfield)

Isn't that powerful? Taking 100% responsibility gives you the power to *un-create* what's not working and *re-create* what you really want!

Living the way of The One invites you to view your life from this perspective. Owning your life and taking 100% responsibility for all that is occurring in your life right now. Find your life perfect right now in this moment. Whether you have tons of money in the bank or you're wondering how you'll pay your bills. Whether you have an awesome marriage or are feeling sad and lonely. You now have the opportunity to take control of the situation and *un-create* what now exists that you don't want and *re-create* what you do want.

There are only three things that we can control in our lives:

1. The thoughts we think,
2. The images we visualize, and
3. The actions we take.

From this place of taking ownership of what you can control, you give yourself permission to dream, to grow and to live a life in alignment with your purpose, values and goals.

Tips for Taking 100% Responsibility

Tip #1: Give Up Blaming.

Become aware of your own behaviors in blaming and complaining.

"All blame is a waste of time. No matter how much fault you find with another and regardless of how much you blame him, it will not change you."
~ Jack Canfield

The only thing you can change is yourself. Be mindful in your conversation and notice your thought patterns. When something is not going right or as planned, are you blaming someone else, are you playing the victim? Do you hear yourself saying, "I don't have any control over the situation" or "I can't believe s/he did that?"

When we stop blaming it allows us to take control. One of my favorite prayers is the Serenity Prayer:

God grant me the serenity to accept the things I cannot change, the courage to change the things I can and the wisdom to know the difference.

Stepping away from that blame and looking at what we can change allows us to move out of the problem and into the solution.

Tip #2: Give Up Complaining.

Now I get that sometimes complaining just feels good. And when you're upset about something, it's good to get it out of your system. The key here is to complain to the right person. Either the person who has authority to change the situation, or someone who will allow you to vent but not travel down the rabbit hole with you! You want to vent to someone who will let you get the stress or frustration out of your system so you can move into the solution. Resist the temptation to vent to someone who will stir up the drama with you, which moves you further from the solution.

Complaining by its very nature in finding dissatisfaction with the way something is, means that you believe there is another way that could be better.

The question then becomes, what are you willing to do about it?

Making a change to the current situation can involve risk to the status quo and you may have to face some consequences or opposition to make that change. Requesting change may involve difficult conversations where people's feelings could be hurt, but solely complaining about a situation without making some effort for corrective measures will do nothing to move you closer to the ideal life that you're now creating.

Pay attention to your conversation and thought patterns. If you are starting to complain about something pause and ask yourself, "What can I change, what can I control in this particular situation?" Then go ahead and take charge of that. If it's something you have no control over, then the only thing you can control is how you respond to the situation.

Principle: 5

Never, Never, Never Gossip

This brings us back to the guiding principle of verbal harmlessness referenced in Principle 3. When people gossip or speak badly about others it does less damage to the reputation of the person they're speaking about than it does to their own reputation.

"Any fool can criticize, condemn and complain–
and most fools do."
~ Dale Carnegie

While it may be tempting to discuss or focus on what appear to be mistakes or bad behavior of others, what gossiping really does is to serve as a distraction from examining yourself and your own behaviors.

Gossiping about others often has its roots in our own feelings of jealousy, insecurity, inadequacy or fear. Before you speak about someone else (especially if they are not present), ask yourself the following questions:

- Would I say what I'm about to say directly to the person I'm speaking about?

- Is what I'm about to say hurtful, unkind or necessary?

- What am I feeling about what the other person did (or said)? Are there any traces of that behavior within myself?

Another factor that makes gossiping attractive and sadly, far too common, is a phenomenon known as *shadenfreude:* a feeling of enjoyment that comes from seeing or hearing about the troubles of other people. Clearly TV executives recognize this and feed the shadenfreude frenzy with programs that depict the lives of others so that mainstream can watch and say, "Whew! Would you look at *them*?" After all, it's easier to look at someone else's life than to examine our own.

As you incorporate the way of The One into your life, talking less and listening more, holding and sharing your vision, being exemplary in your own behavior, and owning your life by taking 100% responsibility, the desire or need to gossip about others will be released.

If you find yourself in a discussion and the conversation turns to gossiping about others, do your best to find something positive to say about the person, change the subject or leave the conversation. Silence can be interpreted as agreement. Speak your mind from a place of kindness and integrity and remove yourself from the discussion.

Remember always that until you walk a mile in someone else's shoes, you really don't know how their feet feel.

Principle: 6

Exercise Your Mind & Spirit: Develop & Grow Daily

To fully embrace the way of The One requires a commitment to continuously exercising your mindset mastery muscles. It has taken you years to create the habits, patterns and belief systems that have been running the show and it will take time and consistency to refine or replace those old patterns. The good news is that your desire, coupled with a commitment to living the way of The One, will support you in peeling away the layers to reveal the extraordinary person you already are!

"Life is a classroom, only those who are willing to be lifelong learners will move to the head of the class."
~ Zig Ziglar

I share with you here the practices and systems that have personally worked for me as well as for thousands of my clients. These practices were developed over years of intense study with mentors, sages and coaches.

I, too, continue to grow and evolve and am committed to sharing what I learn to support and empower others.

I invite you now to seize the opportunity you have before you to experience life and the way of The One using the tools and resources provided and to continue to surround yourself with like-minded and like-spirited people.

Through all phases I encourage you to be patient, persistent and consistent. It has often been said that "success leaves clues." These are the success clues that I have personally used and shared with my clients to support them in living the way of The One and experiencing the magic that it brings.

Daily Practices

Here is my mantra:

Every day I read, write and focus on my vision and my purpose.

"Every day? Really?"
Yes.

"Weekends too?"
Yes.

"What about my birthday?"
Yes.

"How about when I'm on vacation?"
Yes.

"My day is already so full! How will I fit this in?"
It's easy & I'll show you how!

I have been consistently practicing this for close to 20 years. Admittedly, especially in the beginning, there were times when I fell out of practice. As I reflect over the years, it is crystal clear that the times when I have experienced the most success, happiness and prosperity have been when I was fully committed to this practice. I invite you to join me now and dive in to enjoy the rewards that come from consistent and persistent attention to your purpose, your vision and living the way of The One.

Exercise #1: Start Your Day with Gratitude

Before you even get out of bed or lift your head off the pillow, think of 5 people and/or things that you're grateful for. As you consider each one, really spend time thinking in depth about each one. Why are you grateful for this person or thing? What else can you find to be grateful for today? Is it the fact that you have a pillow? Your family (name them one by one), friends, pets, new car, old car that still works and gets you where you want to go, your health, new

opportunities, new shoes, any shoes at all?
"I cried because I had no shoes,
then I met a man who had no feet."
~ Persian Sufi Proverb

There is always something that we can find to be grateful for. All too often people start their day thinking about their long "To Do" list or all of the things that are going wrong, which then sends them in a tailspin of worry, concern and fear. When you start your day with gratitude you'll never wake up on the wrong side of the bed again!

Take a few minutes and list the people and things you are most grateful for right now (remember to *really feel* the appreciation):

(1)

(2)

(3)

(4)

(5)

Nancy Matthews

"Of all the virtues, gratitude is probably the most neglected and least expressed."
~ *John Maxwell*

Exercise #2: Read, Write and Focus on Your Vision Every Day (In Writing)

To begin, keep it simple and commit to a minimum of 15 minutes a day for this practice. Ideally I suggest that you make this the first 15 minutes of your day. And, yes, that may mean waking up 15 minutes earlier. If you feel any resistance to this suggestion, ask yourself: "Is my vision worth getting up 15 minutes earlier?" (I bet you would wake up earlier to catch a flight for a vacation.)

The power of doing this exercise early in your day allows you to set the tone and direction of your attitude for the day and as a result, for the quality of your life.

When you begin your day by checking your email, phone messages and jumping into social media, you instantly shift your focus away from *your* intentions, desires and goals and are instead focusing on the requests and demands of others. This puts you in a state of reaction (or sometimes over-reaction) and you have moved away from your true power of creation.

Bonus Resource:
FREE Audio Download
"The 7 Step System to
Be a Powerful Creator"
➔ NancyMatthews.com/Creator

Suggested Reading: The types of books and magazines to read during this portion of the practice should deal with self-development, positive thinking, leadership, stories of champions who overcame obstacles, and biographies of people you admire and respect. Many people are already reading the Bible as part of their daily practice and by all means continue that practice. What I'm suggesting is that you add another dimension to your personal development through reading other types of books.

Note: It was during my morning time of reading and being focused on my vision (helping others, making more money and expanding my business), that the inspiration to create my first book *Visionaries with Guts* as a compilation was born. The results of this daily practice in just this one instance were amazing:

- Income of over $20,000 in 20 days.

- Providing a vehicle for 27 other people to share their message and become published authors.

- An amazing resource for every reader to tap into their own power as a "Visionary with Guts."

- The perfect resources and connections, The Ones, who helped me take this book from concept to publication in just two short months!

Suggested Writing: Does your mind go blank at the thought of journaling? Do you love to write and could spend hours writing? Whether you're taking on journaling for the first time or have been doing so for years, the way of The One includes being specific and intentional in your journaling. Following these journal guidelines will allow you to get laser focused, develop your vision and experience the magic of living the way of The One.

Ideas to Inspire Your Journaling

Use each of these journal prompts for several consecutive days (or longer). I enjoy variety in my journaling and use these types of prompts on a rotational basis.

Journal Prompt #1
The Six Major Areas of Life:
Choose what you want to create in your day in the areas of:

Body
Mind
Spirit
People
Money
Time

For example, a journal entry could be:

"Today I nourish my body with healthy foods and move my body with 30 minutes of exercise. My mind is active and plentiful, creating new and exciting ideas, my faith is strong and supports me in all areas, I am a people and money magnet, bringing the perfect situations to move me closer to my goals and I handle everything I am meant to with grace and ease."

Put some attention on each of these areas and choose what YOU want to create. What are your heart's desires? Perhaps you desire a quiet mind, a strong lean body, an overflowing bank account. Remember, everything that matters begins in the heart (desire), and then moves to the mind where thoughts become things!

Journal Prompt #2
Yesterday's Lesson and Yesterday's Gifts:
This exercise allows us to recognize and remember that all of our experiences are designed to teach us lessons and keep us in a spirit of gratitude. Review your previous day and answer these questions in your journal:

- What did I learn yesterday? Some new piece of information, something about myself, something to move my business forward?

- What were the best things that happened yesterday? A call from a friend, a new client, waking up feeling refreshed and energized?

- What is The One thing I did today that brought me the most joy, a feeling of being happy or a sense of accomplishment? All too often we focus on the things we didn't do rather than those that we did. Take a moment to give yourself a daily pat on the back. You'll like the way it feels and this will encourage similar behavior and action in the future to elicit the same feeling.

Journal Prompt #3
Gratitude from A to Z: A 26-day Exercise.

Start day one by listing 5 people or things that begin with the letter "A", next day "B", then "C" and so on. Get creative, have fun! (I am grateful for xylophones; they have such a great sound!)

Bonus Resource:
To share in the energy and vibration of gratitude, join the Facebook Group "Gratitude from A to Z"

Exercise #3: Daily Activity (After Journaling)

Set Your Intention: Take a few minutes after journaling to set your intention for the day, remembering what you think about comes about.

- Imagine how your day is going to be.

- How you will feel throughout the day (happy, excited, joyful in expectation of a miracle).

- What type of people will you encounter?

- What type of conversations will you have?

- If you're tackling a big project, how will your mind take on the project? (i.e. I easily go through the updates for my website and my creativity flows effortlessly.)

- If you already have a clear vision and goals that you are working towards, spend some time imagining your big Vision as your reality. Really feel it, see all the people around you, where you are living, where you are travelling. It's time to DREAM BIG!

- Pretend that it's the day after your big goal is achieved. How do you feel? What did you do to achieve the goal and how do you feel about that part of it? Who are the people you're now with and The Ones who helped you along the way? Who are The Ones you served in turning your vision into your reality?

Part Two

Inside, Outside &
Living The Way of The One

What will you do today to make it The One day that makes all the difference?

Today is the day before the tomorrow that can make all your dreams come true. Treat today as The One that will make all the difference. If you put off for tomorrow what you could have done today, you may find you'll end up with nothing but a bunch of empty yesterdays.

Do you realize that every day has the potential to be The One that will transform your life, have your wildest dreams come true and give you the feeling of excitement, fulfillment and joy that you so desire?

Just think…

The day before Jim Carrey landed his first big acting role, he was pretty much an unknown. The day before Thomas Edison and his team developed the working light bulb, they were still in the dark. The day before Susan Boyle sang on American Idol she had nothing but a dream.

We've all been told that life can change in an instant:

- The instant you check your lottery number to find you're a winner.

- The instant you pick up the phone and learn of the passing of a dear friend.

- The instant your baby arrives in the world.

- The instant you're standing in line at the post office and the person in front of you is The One.

"I was standing in line at the post office holding a heavy box of sneakers that I was sending to children in Ghana. I had just returned

from a trip to Ghana where I stayed at an orphanage for 2 weeks and fell in love with the children. I returned from this mission trip with a mission on my heart to continue helping these children. My friend, Gloria Ramirez and I joined forces and began a project to help them. As I was standing in the long line at the post office, the box was cumbersome and heavy and I accidently bumped into the woman in front of me. As she turned to me I immediately apologized and with a warm, beautiful smile she said, "That's alright. Let me help you put the box up on this counter." Filled with appreciation and applying The One Philosophy, we began a conversation which quickly led to me sharing my vision about the children and Ghana."Well, isn't this interesting" she said. "I go to Ghana regularly and know several people in the government, perhaps I can help." ~ Joy Vodofsky, , Glorious Being Center

Yes, The Ones are everywhere – even in the post office! The way to see them is by living the principles of the way of The One.

The One Applied

I am the luckiest girl in the world! Every time I go out to eat at a restaurant I have the best experience and always get the best service! You may think that's a bold statement (or perhaps you wonder if it's really true) and I affirm – it is absolutely true and I know it will continue to be true because I am in control of making it happen. Here's how I do it and how you can too!

It all starts with attitude and here's my going out to eat attitude. Of course, at the base of all my interactions is being The One for others.

I enter the restaurant and when greeted by the hostess who opens the door for me I actually look at him/her and say "Thank you so much." Not just thank you as if by robotic auto pilot programming, I mean "Thank you...how considerate of you to hold the door for me." I actually pause and feel appreciation.

Next, we're seated at the table and the server comes over and I immediately ask their name and then share my name as well as the names of the people I'm with. Then I find something to appreciate about them. It could be their smile, their great energy, a pin on their shirt … something to create a more personal experience between us in that moment … something to create a connection.

In that instant a shift is created by simply taking a moment to be The One to appreciate this person and remind them that they matter and are appreciated. From that point forward we are now sharing a dining experience. Time and time again conversations at the table come from a higher place of joy, laughter and connectivity.

Recently as I was having dinner with my family, my 7-year old grandson shared that he liked break-dancing at the same time that the server was at our table. She chimed in and said, "There's a great dance studio across the street, my daughter takes break-dancing classes there!" Within 2 days my grandson was enrolled and dancing up a storm. Little dreams come true too – and so quickly when you practice The One Philosophy!

There's a secondary benefit to this fun restaurant experience ... the expression on the faces of the people that I'm eating with who catch the fever and go on to be The One when they go out to eat.

Take the restaurant challenge and have every dining experience from here on out be the best ever!

The Ripple Effect

I have been teaching and sharing The One Philosophy for several years as part of my presentations. During the early portion of the events, I share The One Philosophy to create a shift in perspective to place the focus and intention on being The One rather than finding The One. They are reminded that every person is The One and that the portal of possibilities is opened by being The One.

Over the years I have received hundreds of testimonials and stories from people who have embraced The One Philosophy. They share how this fresh perspective and new awareness of hope, possibility and synchronicity has impacted their lives.

Enjoy the stories that follow and see yourself creating your own ripple effect as The One Philosophy becomes totally ingrained in your way of being. That is, being The One!

The Car Accident

"I was driving home from the store listening to The One Philosophy CD in my car. All of a sudden I got hit from behind and then my car slammed into the car in front of me. Fortunately, none of us were going too fast and the amount of damage was minimal. As I was getting out of my car, I thought, "What a great opportunity for me to practice being The One." Rather than immediately jumping to anger, blame or upset, I chose in that moment to come from love for all the people involved. (It was, after all, an 'accident.')

As one of the drivers exited his vehicle I discovered it was an old friend and we greeted each other warmly. I shared a couple of things I was grateful for and the other drivers started chiming in, adding to the gratitude list. What could have been negative was transformed into a pleasant experience for all of us. Being The One is always the way to show up."

~ Kathryn A. Hathaway
The Phoenix Solutions Lawyer

When The One You *Think* Is The One Is Actually The One to Lead You To The Real One

"I thought The One person who could help me get the opportunity I wanted was Jack Canfield. I was on Jack Canfield's website, trying to figure out how I could attend Jack's Breakthrough to Success event in Arizona, when I found out that Jack only had three public events this year and one of them was right here where I live in West Palm Beach, Florida. I signed-up for a VIP ticket so I would be sure to meet The One, Jack Canfield at Women's Prosperity Network's 4th Annual Prosperity UN-Conference.

As the time for the conference came near, I began to embrace my own true vision and I no longer wanted to talk to Jack about an opportunity. I wanted to pursue my real dreams. Jack was The One for me. He was The One who led me to Women's Prosperity Network and Nancy Matthews, The Ones who inspired and empowered me to write the book I have been talking about writing since I was six years old. Nancy Matthews is The One who has been there to share her knowledge and marketing genius, provide constant training and consistent reinforcement to help make my vision a reality.

I have written my book, *Happy in Love: A Woman's Guide to Love, Attraction, Dating and Relationships* in just two months. I am going to launch the Book and the website in January. Then, I will get to be The One to inspire and empower millions of women to love themselves, love their lives and be truly happy in love."

~ Kelley Chappell, PhD

www.HappyinLove.com

It's All About ONE

"Have you ever felt lost, not knowing who you were, where you belonged, or what you were supposed to do next with your life? When my mother became critically ill and was only expected to live 3 weeks, I decided to become The One for her and became her caretaker. She moved into my home and my main focus became being The One for her. Gratefully, those three weeks turned *into 15 quality months of additional life for her and our family. Shortly after she died, I realized that my purpose was no longer being The One for her, but I didn't know what my purpose was, who I was supposed to be and what I was going to do next. Having been The One for my mother for so long left me feeling lost after she was gone.*

I decided to dedicate myself to my business and found myself feeling totally inadequate unskilled, confused and depressed. I was still lost. In a moment of desperation, having heard about a free tele-class led by Gloria Ramirez, I dialed in and stayed on the line, despite the fact that I had difficulty hearing and could only really grasp a portion of what she was saying. What I did hear and understand was that I needed to remember who I was at the core and reconnect with that first, and in that moment I "Found" myself again. Gloria became The One for me that day and many days that followed.

I began with a clean slate and embarked on the next part of my journey, writing my own story and starring in it, utilizing and sharing my gifts, talents and treasures. Embracing The One that I am first which creates the space for me to be The One for others. It all starts with ONE …

> *ONE Decision*
> *ONE Choice*
> *ONE Moment of Courage*
> *ONE Act of Kindness*

The One Can Change Your Life and…
Create a Huge Ripple Effect
Be "The ONE" for someone today!"
> *~ Susan Wiener*

(My wise, kind, gorgeous and wonderful sister, Co-Founder of Women's Prosperity Network.)

Searching for The One

"I have been searching for The One for many years. For a while in my childhood I thought my father, Rabbi Morris Skop was The One I was looking for. He taught me about God and Judaism. He allowed me to question some of his beliefs and traditions and others not so much. I

thought my mother was The One. She was beautiful and an artist. She was a great cook, only she could be mean at times. She was judgmental, especially of me.

I went to school and graduated from the University of Miami and became a teacher. I got married to the man I thought was The One. He gave me two beautiful children only he was very angry and abusive to me at times and we divorced after 11 years of marriage. After my divorce I started looking for The One in bars and night clubs thinking that I would attract Mr. Right. I went to therapy with a psychiatrist thinking he could help me find The One. I was sure there was something wrong with me and I wanted him to dig it out of me.

After 6 years of being single and raising my 2 little children mostly by myself, I started looking for The One in self help books. I read everything from Dr. Nathaniel Branden's <u>Psychology of Self Esteem</u> to Dr. Wayne Dyer's <u>Your Erroneous Zones</u>. I read a lot! Finally in 1997 I married my current husband, Will, and we went on this journey together. In 1981 when I *took Insight Seminars I met Jack Canfield and I thought he was The One who could give me self-esteem and value. In fact he did give me encouragement and support to pursue my dreams of becoming an author and teacher extraordinaire.*

When I was introduced to Women's Prosperity Network and met Nancy Matthews and her sisters, Trish Carr and Susan Wiener, I was introduced to The One Philosophy and given the opportunity to meet wonderful women and men who also were pursuing their missions and dreams.

It was then that I finally realized that I could stop looking for The One. I was The One and so are you and so is each and every one of us! By sharing who I am with others, I have been told that I am an inspiration. And so are you! You inspire me as well. That is my story and I'm sticking with it."

~ Gramma Shirah,
Shirah Penn, M.Ed.

Being The One Makes
Me Feel Good

"For many of us, it's not easy to remember that we are inherently worthy. We are born worthy as a child of God, Goddess, the Universe or whatever you call the infinite power. We are inherently worthy. And instead of knowing that and believing it, we often judge our value from outside ourselves - by how many friends we have, what kind of job we hold, the car we drive or how many 'likes' we have on Facebook.

The One Philosophy reminds me of my inherent value, of my worth, of who I am. The One Philosophy reminds me that I am The One for someone every single day. Whether I smile at a stranger or offer advice to a colleague, I am The One. When I come from knowing that and believing in myself, it makes me actually show up as The One. It boosts my confidence and makes me feel good knowing that I'm of service, that I contribute, that I matter and that doggone it, people like me simply for the magnificent me I am. The One Philosophy reminds me to show up authentically, confidently and open to possibilities. In a word, it's joyful."

~ *Trish Carr*

(My extraordinary, brilliant, beautiful and talented sister, Co-Founder of Women's Prosperity Network.)

Relationships Are More Significant

"Before I learned and understood The One Philosophy as Nancy Matthews has distinguished it, it existed. What Nancy has done is to bring the philosophy into the light so you can identify and recognize it and look for it in each encounter you have with another, either in your personal life or in your business life.

After having met Nancy Matthews and hearing of this philosophy, I was able to look back and recognize just such a person in my life. A person who after I met her, so much flowed for me in my life. The person, The One, is Cheri Martin. She is a business professional I originally met through a seminar she was giving. Eventually I hired Cheri to assist me with social media for my business.

That is not what made Cheri The One. Cheri introduced me to Women's Prosperity Network and to Nancy Matthews and her co-founding sisters, Trish Carr and Susan Weiner. From this introduction to WPN has flowed personal growth, a set of new wonderful relationships that are always expanding and direct business growth and profit. Cheri for me, at that moment, was The One.

I am thankful that Nancy has brought forward this wonderful philosophy that we can, if we choose, incorporate into our daily lives. Knowing and understanding The One Philosophy changes how you interact with others, each person you meet you treat as that special One. They may be The One for you, or you may be The One for them, either way it makes each person special and privileged in your life and your life and relationships are the more magnificent for it."

~ Merinda Crowder,
Luxury & Fine Home Specialist

Endless Possibilities

"The One Philosophy for me means acting as if and believing that every person I meet is The One and learning how we can impact each other.

Since learning about, recognizing and utilizing this awesome way to live, I have effected, and been affected by people who before may have slipped through my life, missing out on the possibilities and results we have created by simply being aware of how we can touch each other in a meaningful way.

Now, being aware of each person and applying The One Philosophy, I have shared more smiles to change the day of a stranger, positively impacted those I care strongly about and forged business partnerships with individuals who may have been just another face in the room.

My business has grown forcefully. Just this week, a team partner told me that she was awed by how my positive leadership has impacted her. Internally, I have become more confident when being with all folks, smiling as if they are The

One, as they just may be!"
~ Diane Chasick,
LifefeSmile Healthy Living

Accepting and Welcoming Others

"I was introduced to The One Philosophy by Nancy Matthews a couple of years ago. Its concept is that you treat everyone with respect. Maybe that person is in your life to help you or, on the other hand, maybe you could help them. It puts a spin on meeting people. I know to welcome others into my life with acceptance knowing that each person is there for a reason. Maybe The One Philosophy is to open my heart more!"

~ Carol Y. Morrgan,
The Dream Lady

Nancy Matthews

The Star Thrower

"Once, on ancient Earth, there was a human boy walking along a beach. There had just been a storm, and starfish had been scattered along the sands. The boy knew the fish would die, so he began to fling the fish to the sea. But every time he threw a starfish, another would wash ashore.

An old Earth man happened along and saw what the child was doing. He called out, 'Boy, what are you doing?' 'Saving the starfish!' replied the boy. 'But your attempts are useless, child! Every time you save one, another one returns, often the same one! You can't save them all, so why bother trying? Why does it matter, anyway?' called the old man.

The boy thought about this for a while, a starfish in his hand; he answered, "Well, it matters to this one." And then he flung the starfish into the welcoming sea."

~Loren Eiseley

Conclusion

Embrace The One Philosophy.

Remember YOU Are The One who has the power to transform each and every interaction by BEING The One for others.

Whether it's someone you meet at a party, a networking event, standing in line at the post office or at a restaurant, treat each and every person you meet as The One…because they are!

Imagine a world where we all treat each other with this level of excitement, enthusiasm and respect.

A world where people are living the way of The One:

- Talking Less and Listening More

- Holding Their Vision and Sharing It With Others

- Exhibiting Exemplary Behavior

- Owning Their Lives By Taking 100% Responsibility

- Never, Never, Never Gossiping

- Exercising Their Minds & Spirits: Developing & Growing Daily

That's the world I want to live in. That's the world I'm creating, day by day, one human interaction, one starfish at a time.

Will The One Philosophy save all the starfish?

I believe it's possible.

It's possible and it's happening right now as you embrace The One Philosophy and share it with all the starfish on your beach.

About The Author

Nancy Matthews is known as *The Visionary with Guts* for her perseverance and commitment in overcoming obstacles, challenges and distractions in achieving her goals. She teaches the leadership, mindset and marketing strategies that allowed her to grow from a struggling single mom living paycheck to paycheck, into a successful business owner, proud parent, respected leader and sought after speaker.

Author of *Visionaries with Guts* and creator of the highly acclaimed Receiving Your Riches Course, Nancy is often featured in the media and has shared the stage with some of today's leading experts on business and transformation.

Founder of Women's Prosperity Network (WomensProsperityNetwork.com), Talk Show Host, Speaker and Master Coach, Nancy works with individuals and organizations to support them in bringing their visions to life.

Special Thanks

Heartfelt thanks to the thousands of people who have embraced and shared The One Philosophy and encouraged me to write this book.

To my children, Zack and Megan, thank you for keeping me humble and giving me the greatest joy of all...being your Mom.

To my sisters, Susan Wiener and Trish Carr, thank you for believing in me and contributing so much value to every aspect of my life.

To my coach, my mentor, my friend, Duane Dale Cummings, "The Sensational Guy," thank you for continuously holding the vision of the big impact contained in this little message and for being The One on so many levels.

To The Ones who shared their stories, thank you for your honesty, your heart and your commitment to being The One and bringing more light and love into our world.

Continue the Journey

Enjoy these plentiful resources to support you in living the way of The One!

FREE Resources!
Go to: **NancyMatthews.com**

FREE Weekly Tele-Class featuring top experts and trusted authorities since 2010 to keep you up to date and in the know for winning in business and in life.
Go to:
WomensProsperityNetwork.com/wow

"Receiving Your Riches", a unique study and guide through *The Science of Getting Rich."* A guided 30-day course to support you in receiving your riches now!
Go to: **NancyMatthews.com/Science**

Contact: **Nancy@NancyMatthews.com**
800-928-6928